THE FULL OUT®
APARTMENT INVESTOR

A COMPREHENSIVE GUIDE FOR
CANADIAN INVESTORS

Mark Faris
and John Makarewicz

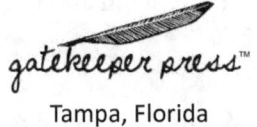

Tampa, Florida

The content associated with this book is the sole work and responsibility of the author. Gatekeeper Press had no involvement in the generation of this content.

The Full Out® Apartment Investor: A Comprehensive Guide for Canadian Investors

Published by Gatekeeper Press
7853 Gunn Hwy., Suite 209
Tampa, FL 33626
www.GatekeeperPress.com

Copyright © 2024 by Mark Faris and John Makarewicz
All rights reserved. Neither this book, nor any parts within it may be sold or reproduced in any form or by any electronic or mechanical means, including information storage and retrieval systems, without permission in writing from the author. The only exception is by a reviewer, who may quote short excerpts in a review.

The cover design for this book is entirely the product of the author. Gatekeeper Press did not participate in and is not responsible for any aspect of that element.

Library of Congress Control Number: 2023948654

ISBN (paperback): 9781662944444

The Full Out ® Apartment Investor

Contents

Chapter 1: Introduction	1
Chapter 2: Your 'Why' Behind Investing and Your Personal Financial Goals	5
Chapter 3: What is Apartment Group Investing?	9
Chapter 4: Deep Dive into the Value-Add Strategy	13
Chapter 5: Expected Returns on a Real Estate Investment Deal	17
Chapter 6: Understanding the Accredited Investor and Its Importance	21
Chapter 7: Vetting Your Real Estate Operating Partner	25
Chapter 8: Choosing the Right Market to Invest In	29
Chapter 9: Defining the Four Different Multifamily Apartment Asset Classes	33
Chapter 10: Shortage of Workforce and Affordable Housing	37
Chapter 11: Reading and Understanding the Investment Offering Summary	41
Chapter 12: Navigating the Private Placement Memorandum	45
Chapter 13: Avoiding Dual Taxation While Investing in the US Market	47
Chapter 14: Tax Benefits of Investing in an Apartment Group Investment	49
Chapter 15: Why Work with Faris Capital Partners	51

Chapter 1

Introduction

If there's one thing I hear over and over again in my role as a real estate professional, it's a simple statement filled with regret: "I wish I had invested more of my money in real estate."

So why do people feel this way? It comes down to a few key reasons.

Firstly, real estate is a fantastic hedge against inflation. While the value of money can be eroded by inflation, real estate typically increases in value over time and keeps pace with or even outperforms inflation, maintaining purchasing power and yielding real returns. Secondly, property values generally rise over a long time horizon. Yes, there are market fluctuations, but the overall trajectory is upward, building wealth over time. Finally, when bought smartly, real estate provides better-than-average returns, significantly outpacing traditional investments.

Our mission at Faris Capital Partners is to shed light on an often-overlooked facet of real estate investing, particularly for Canadians: multifamily apartment investing in the United States. You might be wondering why the US, and why, specifically Florida? The US housing market, particularly in areas like Florida, has shown

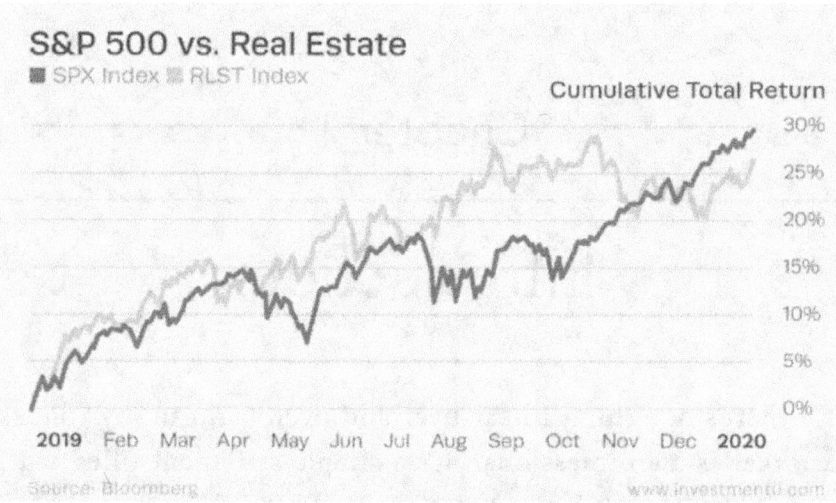

consistent growth, and there's a robust demand for rental properties. Florida also boasts a strong economy, favorable tax climate, and a growing population, making it a prime location for real estate investing. Also, due to high property values, rent controls, and higher interest rates, finding cash-flowing real estate in Canada has become very difficult, if not impossible.

But, you might be asking, what about dual taxation? As a Canadian, wouldn't I be taxed in both countries? Well, this is where it gets interesting. With proper structuring and guidance, you can navigate investing in the US without falling victim to double taxation. More on that later.

Recent market volatility and high inflation are undeniable, making traditional investment strategies like stock market investing unpredictable and fraught with uncertainties. The quest for an investment approach that can weather these economic storms leads us to one powerful solution: investing in apartment buildings.

Why do we believe so strongly in this? Well, regardless of what the stock market does or what the inflation rate is, people always need a place to live. The demand for housing, especially affordable rental housing, stays steady. Due to a variety of factors, including the Great Recession and higher materials costs, many markets in the US have low housing inventory, which makes apartment investing even more appealing. This demand for stability, coupled with the potential for impressive returns, makes investing in multifamily apartment buildings a winning strategy.

Our conviction is rooted in our own personal experiences and the successes we've seen investing in this model. Apartment investing has demonstrated time and time again its ability to protect and grow wealth in a turbulent economy. This isn't just about making money, though. It's about securing your future, achieving financial freedom, and ensuring the well-being of your family for years to come.

In the chapters ahead, we will provide you with an in-depth understanding of apartment group investing and how you can leverage it to your benefit. We believe that with knowledge comes power—the power to make informed decisions, navigate financial turbulence, and take control of your financial future. And that's precisely what we're here to help you do.

In this book, we will cover quite a bit of information. It is important to know that we are always available to talk at Faris Capital Partners. Simply reach out to us to schedule a time to talk. We would be happy to personally discuss anything and everything covered in this book.

Disclaimer:

Please note that the content presented in this book is intended for informational purposes only and represents the research, views, and opinions of Faris Capital Partners. The material provided here should not be regarded as financial or investment advice. Every individual has unique circumstances and goals, and this book does not consider these specific factors. It is strongly recommended that prospective investors seek independent financial and legal advice before making any investment decisions. Any investment involves a degree of risk, including the potential loss of principal. Faris Capital Partners makes no guarantee as to the outcomes of any investment made based on the information presented in this book.

Chapter 2

Your 'Why' Behind Investing and Your Personal Financial Goals

When it comes to making investments, the guiding star should always be your 'why.' It is the foundation of your investment strategy and informs the decisions you make along your financial journey. Are you creating a nest egg for retirement? Dreaming of purchasing a vacation home? Perhaps your sights are set on a steady passive income stream to fund a comfortable retirement. You might be looking to fund a new business venture, or perhaps your ambition leans towards philanthropy, using your wealth for charitable donations. Every investment you make should align with these personal financial goals.

The beauty of investing lies in the diversity of options and strategies available to meet varying financial objectives. All financial planners recommend a diversified investment approach. Do you have real estate in your portfolio?

When investing in real estate, there are three core strategies you might consider:

1. Investing for Cash Flow: This strategy prioritizes properties that generate a steady, reliable stream of income, often through rental returns. It's a fantastic strategy for those looking for an additional income source or to fund their retirement.

2. Investing for Appreciation: Here, the primary goal isn't immediate income but the potential for the property value to increase over time. Properties in rapidly growing or developing areas often fall under this strategy. The end goal? To sell the property at a higher price than what you initially paid.

3. Investing for Cash Flow and Appreciation: The hybrid approach. This strategy seeks to gain the best of both worlds, combining the steady income from rentals with the long-term property value increase. This is the approach we employ at Faris Capital Partners.

Why real estate?

Simply put, it is a tangible asset that appreciates over time and simultaneously produces income. Unlike stocks, bonds, or mutual funds, real estate provides a sense of security and control as you can physically see and touch your investment. Furthermore, it is a reliable hedge against inflation. As the cost of living increases, so does the value of the property and the rental income created from it.

The magic of real estate investment lies in its flexibility. No matter your financial goals or personal 'why,' real estate offers a pathway to help you achieve those goals. So, as you take these steps into the world of multifamily apartment investing, remember to keep your 'why' at the heart of it all. It's not just about building wealth; it's about building the life you want to live.

Chapter 3

What is Apartment Group Investing?

At its heart, apartment group investing is a simple and powerful concept. It's a way for a group of individuals to pool their resources together and achieve something far greater than they could alone. Let's break it down and see how it works.

In an apartment group investment deal, there are typically two key roles: the investor or Limited Partner (LP), and the sponsor or General Partner (GP). As an investor or Limited Partner, your role is straightforward and passive: you're providing the capital necessary for the investment deal. You're the fuel that powers the engine.

The sponsor or General Partner, on the other hand, is like the driver of the vehicle. They're the ones who locate a promising property, acquire it, manage it, and ultimately, sell it. They're making the day-to-day decisions, navigating the market fluctuations, and steering the investment toward profitability.

One strategy that a General Partner may employ is known as a 'value-add' strategy. This is where we at Faris Capital Partners shine. In a value-add strategy, the aim is to locate an underperforming property—a diamond in the rough, if you will. It's a property with potential that hasn't been fully realized yet. Perhaps it needs renovations, better operations, or improved management. No matter the circumstances, Faris Capital Partners will operate with excellence to ensure maximum financial returns.

By investing capital into these improvements, the value of the property can be significantly increased. This, in turn, allows for higher rental rates and, ultimately, a more profitable investment. It's the process of creating value where there is untapped potential, making the pie bigger for everyone involved.

There's also another strategy called opportunistic investments. This involves looking for severely underperforming or change in use assets, such as hotel and office conversions. These properties might be dated, in rough condition, or located in challenging areas. The risk is undeniably higher with these properties, but so is the potential reward. It's the proverbial 'fixer-upper' on steroids.

However, at Faris Capital Partners, we're focused on value-add strategies. We believe that this approach offers the best balance of risk and reward, providing our investors with stable, attractive returns. Our expertise lies in identifying these underperforming properties, unlocking their potential, and transforming them into high-performing assets.

By participating in an apartment investment deal, you get the best of both worlds. You're able to benefit from the substantial returns that real estate investing can offer without the need to become a real estate expert or a full-time landlord yourself. You contribute the capital, and we handle the rest. It's a partnership that has the potential to deliver a future of financial stability and growth. Let's explore this fascinating world further in the upcoming chapters.

Chapter 4

Deep Dive into the Value-Add Strategy

The Value-Add Strategy is an approach that forms the backbone of our investing philosophy at Faris Capital Partners. This strategy involves taking an existing property and enhancing its value through a variety of improvements and management efficiencies. However, the application of a value-add strategy isn't simply about making cosmetic changes; it involves a series of strategic decisions and precise execution.

Let's delve a little deeper.

At the core of our value-add strategy is what we call the "Full Out 28-Day Property Transformation." Think of it as a high-speed renovation blitz that rapidly transforms the property. We focus on the exteriors, the common areas, and the overall aesthetics of the complex. Within twenty-eight days of taking ownership, we paint the exterior, overhaul the landscaping, update the leasing office, refresh the amenity furniture, and replace signage. These actions are aimed at quickly enhancing the property's curb appeal, making it more attractive to potential tenants, and improving the environment for existing ones.

But our improvements don't stop at the property's exterior. As tenants move out or their leases end, we renovate their units. These renovations might include new flooring, upgraded kitchen countertops, fresh paint, and updated hardware as needed. This not only increases the value of each individual unit but also allows us to command higher rents, further driving the profitability of the property.

Here's a neat trick we've found: success in incentivizing our existing tenants to move into these renovated units. This accomplishes two things. First, it increases tenant satisfaction, as they get to live in a newly renovated unit, and we get to enjoy higher rent for the same tenant. Second, it allows us to renovate more units faster, accelerating the overall improvement of the property.

However, none of these steps would be effective without strict project management. Our team is on the ground, tightly managing the construction teams. At a minimum, we have weekly meetings with them, to ensure that the renovation process stays on track and that the quality of work remains high. We also regularly visit the property to confirm everything is on schedule and to hold the construction team accountable. On the procurement side, we work tirelessly to source the highest quality materials at the lowest possible prices, optimizing our renovation budgets for maximum impact.

Physical transformations only form one part of the value-add equation. We're just as committed to implementing tighter financial controls and identifying additional income opportunities. We renegotiate service contracts to ensure cost-effectiveness and explore revenue-boosting ventures such as assigned parking, the construction of for-rent storage units, or the addition of a coin-operated laundry facility. We also create revenue-sharing arrangements with utility providers, where possible. These are just some of the things we might do, depending on the particular apartment complex.

Additionally, we firmly believe in the importance of superior property management. Our management teams are held accountable for results, maintaining a keen focus on leasing rates, renewal percentages, and overall tenant satisfaction. This hands-on approach ensures not only the smooth day-to-day operation of our properties but also contributes to their long-term financial success. We conduct weekly check-ins with the property management team, holding them accountable to our expectations.

By harnessing this holistic value-add strategy, we successfully turn underperforming properties into thriving communities. It's through this transformation that we increase the value of our properties, providing our investors with superior returns on their investments. This win-win approach benefits everyone involved— our investors enjoy stronger returns, tenants relish in enhanced living spaces, and the wider community benefits from the overall upliftment. It's a testament to the transformative power of strategic investment, meticulous planning, and diligent execution.

Chapter 5

Expected Returns on a Real Estate Investment Deal

In the realm of investing, returns can never be guaranteed. Each investment carries its own unique blend of risks and potential rewards. However, by understanding how returns are structured, you can make informed decisions that align with your personal financial goals.

At Faris Capital Partners, we typically offer a preferred return to our investors of 7%. This means that our investors receive the first 7% of profits from the property before we, as the syndicators, take our share. We believe in the properties we invest in, and to prove it, we personally invest in each deal we make. Our skin is in the game right alongside yours, ensuring that our interests align with our investors.

Of course, not all real estate syndicators offer the same structure. Each operator may have a different investment approach, targeted return, risk profile, or profit-sharing structure. It's crucial that investors perform due diligence and research before making an investment decision.

When we evaluate potential deals, we typically target a cash-on-cash return of 4-6% and an internal rate of return (IRR) in the 15-20% range.

But what do these terms mean?

Cash-on-cash return is a percentage that shows the cash income earned on the cash invested in a property. For instance, if you invested $100,000 into a property and received $8,000 in cash flow over a year, your cash-on-cash return would be 8%.

The internal rate of return, on the other hand, is a metric used in capital budgeting to estimate the profitability of potential investments. IRR is the discount rate that makes the net present value (NPV) of all cash flows (both positive and negative) equal to zero. It's an annualized figure that includes both the profits from operations (cash flow) and the eventual profits from sale, taking into account the time value of money.

Our investment horizon typically ranges from 3 to 5 years, during which we hold properties before refinancing or selling. However, this timeline can vary based on a variety of factors, such as market conditions. Our primary focus is always on maximizing returns for our investors while carefully managing risks.

As with any investment, it's essential to remember that past performance is not indicative of future results. Each deal is unique and requires its own detailed analysis. With careful planning, due diligence, and sound management, multifamily apartment real estate investments can offer attractive opportunities for building wealth.

Chapter 6

Understanding the Accredited Investor and Its Importance

When it comes to investing in certain types of assets, such as real estate group investments, it's essential to understand what it means to be an "accredited investor." In essence, an accredited investor is an individual or a business entity that is allowed to trade securities that may not be registered with financial authorities. The laws of Canada recognize them as being financially sophisticated and with a reduced need for the protection provided by certain government filings.

In Canada, as defined by regulatory bodies, such as the Ontario Securities Commission and the Canadian Securities Administrators, an accredited investor is:

1. An individual who, alone or together with a spouse, owns financial assets worth more than $1 million before taxes but excluding the value of their primary residence.

2. An individual who, alone or together with a spouse, has net assets of at least $5 million.

3. An individual whose net income before taxes exceeded $200,000 in both of the last two years and who expects to maintain at least the same level of income this year.

4. An individual whose net income before taxes, combined with that of a spouse, exceeded $300,000 in both of the last two years and who expects to maintain at least the same level of income this year.

5. An individual who currently is, or once was, a registered advisor or dealer other than a limited market dealer.

Why does being an accredited investor matter when investing in real estate group investment deals?

Real estate group investments often involve unregistered securities. Regulatory bodies set these criteria to ensure that only individuals who are financially experienced and can bear the risk of loss have access to such investment opportunities.

The reason behind these criteria is to protect less experienced investors from potentially complex and risky investments. If you meet the accredited investor criteria, it suggests that you have a strong understanding of investment practices, the associated risks, and that you can withstand potential financial loss. All of our investment opportunities require that the investor be accredited.

By investing in a real estate group investment, you're pooling your resources with other accredited investors to purchase larger properties than you might be able to afford alone, such as multifamily apartment complexes. It's an opportunity to expand your investment portfolio, diversify risk, and potentially realize significant returns on your investment. However, like any investment, it comes with risks that need to be thoroughly understood.

Chapter 7

Vetting Your Real Estate Operating Partner

Before you invest your hard-earned money in a real estate group investment, it's crucial that you conduct thorough due diligence on potential sponsors. Remember, the most crucial aspect of any real estate group investment is the sponsor. Here's what you need to look for and questions to ask:

1. Track Record: A sponsor's track record reveals their level of experience, their ability to handle complex situations, and their past performance. At Faris Capital Partners, we have a stellar track record in the investing and business arena. Mark Faris and John Makarewicz, for instance, scaled two of the largest real estate teams in Canada and the US, respectively, selling over $20 billion in real estate. In apartment group investments, we've completed two acquisitions to date, both of which are performing in line with projections.

Questions to ask: (let's focus on questions that focus on our overall track record in business)
- What is your track record in owning and operating a business?
- How many assets have you acquired?
- Can you provide references from other investors?

2. The Team: Look for a sponsor with an all-star team—one that hires only experienced A-players in their roles.

Questions to ask:
- Who are the key players in your team?
- How long has the team been in place?
- What are their credentials and experience in this field?
- How does your team approach risk management?

3. Trustworthiness: Trusting your sponsor is crucial since you are entrusting them with your investment. It's essential to feel comfortable with their integrity, transparency, and commitment to investor interests.

Questions to ask:
- How do you communicate with your investors?
- Can I easily get in touch with the team if I have questions or concerns?
- What measures do you have in place to protect investor interests?
- Are you personally investing in your deals?
- What kind of fees are included in the deal?

4. Process and Approach: Understand their investment strategy, underwriting process, risk-mitigation strategies, and how they handle potential problems.

Questions to ask:
- What is your investment strategy?
- Can you walk me through your due diligence process?
- How do you select markets to invest in?
- How do you approach risk-mitigation in your deals?
- How do you handle potential issues or problems that might arise during the investment term?

By asking these questions and conducting thorough due diligence, you can ensure that you choose a sponsor aligned with your investment goals and philosophy. Partnering with the right sponsor, like Faris Capital Partners, can set the stage for a successful and profitable real estate group investment.

Chapter 8

Choosing the Right Market to Invest In

The journey to successful real estate group investing begins with a critical choice—selecting the right market. This choice requires careful consideration of various factors that collectively influence the viability and potential returns of your investment.

One of the first factors to review is the economic vibrancy of the prospective market. For instance, the population size and growth of an area can significantly affect the demand for housing. Markets experiencing population growth often see a corresponding rise in rental demand, leading to increased rents and property values. However, population growth should be accompanied by economic and population diversity. A market with a variety of job sectors tends to be less vulnerable to economic shifts, offering more stability for your investment. Likewise, a diverse mix of age and income levels among the populace often results in a more stable rental market.

Just as important is the local economic health. Look at the average household income, the income growth trajectory, and the unemployment rate. Markets with higher household incomes and low unemployment usually denote a healthy economy—a positive sign for rental demand and rental rates.

Moving from the broader economic picture, let's zoom into the specific neighborhoods within your chosen market. A neighborhood's character, signaled by crime rates, household income, poverty levels, and local unemployment rates, can affect both property values and the quality of potential tenants. For instance, neighborhoods with lower crime rates are likely to attract higher-quality tenants, and higher neighborhood income usually corresponds to higher potential rents and property values.

Next, you'll want to delve into the specifics of the real estate market. Examine factors such as the ratio of owner-occupied to rental properties, the rent-to-income ratio, the local apartment vacancy rate, and the average rents for the area. Each of these factors can give you insights into rental demand and the potential returns on your investment.

Finally, don't overlook regulatory factors. Local and state laws can influence the cost and ease of property management. Tax rates, insurance costs, and landlord-tenant laws vary widely and can significantly impact your bottom line.

The process of choosing the right market is intricate and requires diligent research. At Faris Capital Partners, we understand the importance of this decision and undertake comprehensive market analysis before selecting a location for our investments. It's all part of our commitment to growing your investment and protecting your capital in a way that aligns with your financial goals and risk tolerance.

Chapter 9

Defining the Four Different Multifamily Apartment Asset Classes

In real estate investing, understanding the different multifamily asset classes is a crucial part of making informed investment decisions. Broadly speaking, properties are categorized into four distinct classes: A, B, C, and D. These classifications are used to denote a property's age, location, amenities, and tenant income level, providing a snapshot of the investment potential and risk profile of each asset.

Class A properties are typically the most coveted among these asset classes. They are generally newer properties, often less than 10 to 15 years old, and located in desirable locations. These apartments are often characterized by high-quality construction and design, boasting a plethora of luxury amenities such as gyms, pools, concierge services, and state-of-the-art appliances. As such, they attract high-income tenants who are willing to pay premium rents for the conveniences and lifestyle they offer. However, due to their already optimized condition and premium pricing, Class A properties often offer lower yields and have less room for value-add strategies.

Class B properties, on the other hand, present an interesting balance of risk and reward. These are usually older than Class A properties, perhaps 20 to 30 years old, but they are still well-maintained and located in good neighborhoods. While they may not have all the luxurious amenities of a Class A property, they often offer solid, comfortable accommodations that appeal to middle-income tenants. The benefit for investors is the potential to implement value-add strategies, such as modernizing units or adding amenities, to increase rents and property value, thereby providing an opportunity for higher yields. Age is definitely a factor if they haven't been modernized and renovated to today's standards.

Class C properties are typically older, often more than 30 years old, and located in less desirable locations. These properties may require more maintenance and offer fewer amenities. However, they also typically command lower rents, making them attractive to lower-income tenants. For investors, the potential returns can be substantial if they're willing to invest in significant renovations and property management to address deferred maintenance and potentially problematic tenant issues. This potential for significant value-add is the key attraction of Class C properties.

Finally, Class D properties are often found in challenging neighborhoods, frequently with higher crime rates. These properties are typically in a state of disrepair and may have significant vacancy issues. They attract low-income tenants and often present more substantial management challenges. While Class D properties can be bought at low prices, they generally require extensive time, effort, and investment to improve their condition and profitability. As such, they are often suitable for more experienced investors with the resources and experience to navigate the complexities associated with these assets.

In summary, each asset class has its unique blend of risks and rewards. At Faris Capital Partners, we typically focus on Class B properties in solid markets. Our goal is to turn that B asset into an A asset through our Full Out Property Transformation Process. We believe these asset classes offer the best opportunity for risk-adjusted returns, allowing us to implement our value-add strategies while providing our investors with consistent cash flow and strong upside potential.

Chapter 10

Shortage of Workforce and Affordable Housing

The shortage of workforce and affordable housing in many markets across North America is a complex issue, deeply rooted in a number of economic factors and market dynamics. The reality is that the demand for affordable places to live, particularly in urban areas and burgeoning job markets, has outpaced the supply, and this trend is likely to continue into the foreseeable future.

One of the key factors contributing to this shortage is the steady rise in housing prices over the past several years. The increased costs of land, labor, and construction materials have driven developers to focus predominantly on luxury or high-end housing, which yields a higher return on investment. The result is a scarcity of new, affordable developments for lower and middle-income families, further exacerbating the imbalance between supply and demand.

Moreover, the growth of the economy, particularly in technology and other high-wage sectors, has driven up the cost of living in certain markets. This economic growth attracts more workers, which in turn, increases the demand for housing. However, the housing market often struggles to keep up with this growing demand, leading to an undersupply of affordable homes and apartments.

Adding to the strain, over the past several decades, we've seen a trend of urbanization, with people moving from rural areas into cities in search of better job opportunities. This influx of people into already densely populated areas puts additional pressure on housing markets.

To further compound the issue, wages for middle- and low-income workers have not kept pace with the rising cost of living. While high-income households have seen substantial wage growth, many workers in lower-wage industries are not earning significantly more than they were decades ago when adjusted for inflation. This wage stagnation makes it increasingly difficult for these individuals to afford housing, especially in markets where housing costs have surged.

Finally, the impact of the global COVID-19 pandemic cannot be understated. The pandemic has caused significant economic upheaval, leading to job loss and income instability for many individuals, which further increased the demand for affordable housing options. Meanwhile, supply chain disruptions and labor shortages have hampered new construction, exacerbating the supply shortage.

As multifamily apartment real estate investors, we recognize the societal and economic implications of this issue. Our investment approach at Faris Capital Partners is centered around identifying undervalued properties in markets with strong growth potential. Through strategic improvements and effective property management, we aim to provide quality, affordable housing options to the workforce population, while also generating solid returns for our investors. It's a win-win scenario that we believe is sustainable, impactful, and profitable.

Chapter 11

Reading and Understanding the Investment Offering Summary

Navigating through an investment offering summary, also known as an offering memorandum, can be an overwhelming task for first-time investors. However, it's an integral part of the investment process that allows you to gauge the viability and potential of the proposed investment.

When you're handed an offering memorandum, the first thing you should look at is the executive summary. This section should provide you with a succinct overview of the entire investment. It typically includes the property's name, location, asking price, financing details, and a high-level summary of the proposed business plan.

Next, you'll find a more detailed presentation of the investment strategy. This might include a thorough explanation of the business plan, proposed renovations or upgrades, and how these actions will add value and generate returns. It should also contain details on the exit strategy, which lays out how and when the property will be sold or refinanced, and how profits will be distributed among investors.

Another crucial component is the financial analysis, which provides a deeper dive into the property's current financial situation and projected financial performance. This typically includes historical and projected income and expense figures, as well as metrics such as the internal rate of return (IRR), equity multiple, and cash-on-cash return. It's important to understand these numbers and ensure they align with your investment goals.

In addition to the financials, the offering memorandum should also contain a market analysis. This section provides insights into the local real estate market, economic trends, and demographic information. It should highlight why the specific market is favorable for real estate investment, and how it's expected to perform in the future.

Finally, the offering memorandum should detail the team behind the project. This section includes biographies of key team members, as well as their track records and relevant experience. The sponsors should have a demonstrated history of successfully executing similar investments.

The offering memorandum is a vital tool for investors to comprehend the nuances of the proposed investment. Therefore, it's crucial to take the time to read and understand it fully. If there are aspects you don't understand, don't hesitate to ask the syndicator for clarification. Remember, investing in real estate deals is not just about the property; it's about having trust in the people who will manage your investment.

Chapter 12

Navigating the Private Placement Memorandum

The private placement memorandum (PPM) is one of the essential documents you'll encounter when investing in a real estate deal. Unlike the offering summary, which highlights the potential of the investment, the PPM focuses on the legal aspects and risks of the investment. It's a detailed document, sometimes running to hundreds of pages, and can be a bit daunting at first glance. However, it's crucial to understand its components and their significance in protecting both the investor and the syndicator.

A PPM typically starts with a summary of the offering, giving you a high-level overview of the investment, including the total raise, minimum investment amount, and the structure of the investment. Following this summary, you'll find a detailed disclosure of the investment's risks. These risks can range from general real estate market risks to those specific to the particular property or its location. This section is designed to ensure that you, as an investor, are fully aware of what can go wrong.

The next section often provides information on the structure of the entity that holds the property, usually an LLC or LP, and the roles of its members. It explains how the profits will be distributed among members, the voting rights of the members, and what happens if a member wants to sell their stake.

The PPM also contains a detailed explanation of the compensation structure for the syndicator or the general partner. This typically includes acquisition fees, asset management fees, and the profit split between the general partner and the limited partners. It's crucial to understand these numbers, as they can significantly impact your returns.

Another critical part of the PPM is the subscription agreement. This section is essentially the contract between you and the syndicator, outlining your commitment to fund a certain amount of the investment.

Lastly, the PPM will include exhibits such as the operating agreement of the LLC, a copy of the title insurance, and the property appraisal or other supporting documents. These add credibility to the facts stated in the PPM and serve as a reference for the investors.

Reading a PPM is not an easy task, but it's crucial to understand it fully before making an investment decision. Consider consulting with a legal or financial advisor who can help navigate through this document and provide sound advice. After all, investing in an apartment complex is a significant commitment, and it's crucial to understand every detail before diving in.

Chapter 13

Avoiding Dual Taxation While Investing in the US Market

As a Canadian investor, you may have concerns about investing in the US due to the potential for dual taxation. Faris Capital Partners, has made this issue a priority, designing a tax-efficient legal structure with the help of experienced tax and legal counsel to ensure our Canadian investors can navigate the cross-border investment landscape with ease.

Our legal structure allows Canadians to invest through a Canadian Limited Partnership rather than a US-based entity. This setup offers several key advantages. First, it opens the doors for any accredited Canadian resident, whether individual or corporation, to invest without the need to create a US entity. This simplifies the process and removes an extra layer of bureaucracy from your investment journey.

Secondly, our structure ensures that the tax you'll be subject to will be the same, regardless of whether the Limited Partnership invests in US or Canadian property. There's no additional tax for venturing into the profitable US markets.

Furthermore, the tax-efficient structure we've designed eliminates the need for tax withholdings, which can sometimes become a source of hassle and confusion for investors. This streamlined approach allows for more straightforward, efficient tax handling.

Finally, our structure ensures that each year, you will receive a T5013 Statement of Partnership Income and Losses. This statement will allocate your share of income and losses based on your ownership percentage. You then report this information on your personal or corporate tax return, depending on your method of investment. This makes your tax reporting process seamless and straightforward.

In short, our structure at Faris Capital Partners is designed with the specific goal of making cross-border investment as hassle-free as possible. We ensure that Canadians can enjoy the fruits of US real estate investment without the extra headache of dual taxation, leaving you to focus on the most important thing: the growth of your wealth.

Chapter 14

Tax Benefits of Investing in an Apartment Group Investment

Investing in a multifamily apartment property carries several substantial tax advantages that can significantly enhance your returns, both during the holding period and upon exit of the investment. This means that, as an investor, you're not only benefiting from potential capital growth and income but also from strategic tax benefits.

During the holding period, the benefits of depreciation and mortgage interest deductions play a vital role. Depreciation, a non-cash expense, allows you to deduct a portion of the property's cost each year, which reduces your taxable income. In an apartment group investment, this benefit is passed on to investors on a proportionate basis, making it a significant tax advantage.

Alongside depreciation, the interest paid on the mortgage loan for the property also provides a tax shield. Since most of the mortgage repayments in the initial years go towards interest, this can be deducted from your taxable income, leading to a further reduction in your tax liability.

Another compelling tax advantage comes from the ability to refinance the property. As the syndicate works to force appreciation of the property and increase its value, you can refinance the investment tax-free. This "cash-out refinance" allows investors to tap into their share of the property's equity growth without incurring additional taxes.

Upon exiting the investment, apartment investing continues to provide tax benefits. The profit from the sale of a property is considered a capital gain, which is typically taxed at a lower rate than ordinary income, leading to tax savings. Furthermore, any capital gains can be offset with capital losses from other investments. This benefit means that if you have other investments that have lost value, these losses can be used to counterbalance your capital gains, potentially lowering your tax liability to zero, depending on the availability of losses you may have.

Overall, multifamily apartment investments offer numerous tax advantages to investors. These benefits go a long way in reducing your overall tax liability while providing additional avenues for wealth creation. Therefore, it's no surprise that savvy investors often choose to invest in multifamily apartments as part of their wealth-building strategies.

Chapter 15

Why Work with Faris Capital Partners

Choosing the right partner for real estate investing is critical for a high-net-worth investor like yourself. With a myriad of options out there, what makes Faris Capital Partners stand out? It boils down to a combination of experience, strategy, and commitment to our investors that sets us apart.

When you're looking for a team to handle your real estate investments, you want proven success and market expertise. At Faris Capital Partners, you get both. Our founders, Mark Faris and John Makarewicz, have a track record that speaks volumes. They scaled the two largest real estate teams in Canada and the US, respectively, selling over $20 billion in real estate. Their experience in multifamily apartment investing is just as compelling, with properties consistently performing on target with projections. We bring this knowledge and track record to every deal we undertake.

Moreover, we believe in the power of a team. Faris Capital Partners only hires the best in the business, creating an all-star lineup that's dedicated to finding and managing the best investment opportunities for you. We've partnered with Djuric Family Office, leveraging their expertise to make informed and wise decisions. The Djuric Family Office is an experienced player in the multifamily apartment space with over 6,400 units owned and over one billion dollars under management. With us, you can be assured of a team that's tirelessly working towards your investment goals.

Understanding the marketplace is another essential element in real estate investing. We leverage cutting-edge technologies and best-in-class market research to identify the most promising markets and opportunities. Currently, our focus is on robust markets such as Orlando, Tampa, and Jacksonville, in the thriving state of Florida. With a diverse job market, strong population growth, and a landlord-friendly environment, these markets offer tremendous potential for investors seeking passive income and strong returns.

Trust is another key aspect of our partnerships. We understand the significance of investing your hard-earned money, and we value the trust you place in us. Our approach to real estate investing is transparent and detail-oriented. We provide in-depth information about every aspect of our deals and are always available for any queries or concerns you might have.

We also understand the importance of risk mitigation in real estate investments. Our Full Out Proven Process helps mitigate risk by ensuring we only pursue the best deals that align with our business plan and your investment goals. Through comprehensive due diligence, regular site visits, and diligent financial analysis, we ensure that every investment is secure and profitable.

Lastly, investing with Faris Capital Partners means being part of our commitment to generating passive income and wealth for our investors. We offer a first-class experience, including a written business plan, webinars, and one-on-ones. We work towards making monthly distributions to our partner investors within six months of acquisition. Our goal is to provide an incredible experience, one that will have you investing with us again and again.

When you partner with Faris Capital Partners, you're choosing more than just a real estate investment company; you're choosing a trusted partner committed to achieving your financial goals. Let's build your wealth together through apartment real estate investing.

www.ingramcontent.com/pod-product-compliance
Lightning Source LLC
LaVergne TN
LVHW011859060526
838200LV00054B/4426